Perfect Daughters
and
Other Fairytales

© 2020 Anastasia Belle Smith

ISBN 978-0-5787-2615-1

All rights reserved.

Let me explain.

I am not perfect. Neither are you. We aren't perfect.

This book has captured some of my angriest moments, some of my darkest, and some of my best. This book isn't supposed to make you feel bad about not being perfect.

It is supposed to make you feel so utterly human that you acknowledge all the cracks and blemishes in yourself and fill them with roses (or whatever you prefer).

Not to glorify them, but to celebrate them.

Because we all wear our bruises differently. Some of us run from our truth,

While others stand in the storm in awe of who they've become and everything they've done.

I've done both.

But recently I have been practicing facing the past. Facing the scars and the things I wish I could change.

Finally, I am reminding myself that it was never my job to be the perfect friend, or sister, or daughter.

It has been my job to learn from my scars. And that's what I have done.

I learned that I will never be perfect, that some things will never completely leave my mind. I have learned that I cannot live another second in fear of what we did.

I learned that perfect daughters are fake.

A perfect daughter is nothing more than a lie:

A goose chase that society has led us on to keep us feeling that we are not enough

Trigger Warning

This collection contains mentions of topics some might consider triggering such as but not limited to...
- Substance Abuse
- Self Harm
- Suicide
- Religion
- Sexual Harassment
- Alcoholism
- Toxic Relationships
- Trauma

Remember to take care of yourself mentally and physically, we need you here.

THE CHARACTERS OF REAL LIFE.

Princess

Evil Witch

Stable Boy

Prince

King

Maiden

The Truth

God

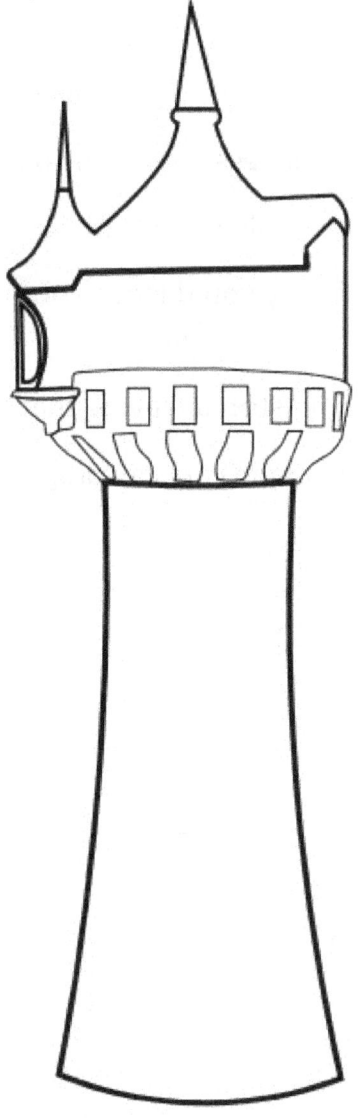

Oh **princess**, how you could

rule the world.

If only you'd leave your tower

and stop believing that

only a man can slay dragons.

WHY ARE WE TAUGHT TO WAIT?

Here are the stages

of being a princess:

Waiting,

Waiting,

Waiting,

Being found by the prince.

Realizing he is human just like you.

Spending the rest of your life

wondering why you waited.

DRAGONS IN MY HEAD

I threw my heart at the wall,

My mind on the floor,

My sanity jumped from the window,

and the voices smiled.

Because they were the only things

I could not shake.

THIS IS FOR ME

I hear your words drift up
into my tower.

And my blood boiled.

But my own need

for peace

kept me at bay.

Princess:

A girl who is waiting

on some boy

to come save her.

Then treats him

like a God

when he finally arrives.

Queen:

A woman who has learned

that not all boys

look in towers.

Witch:

The woman

who had to break

the curse herself

and to find out

she didn't need him

as much as she wanted him.

My heart

won't make room

for any other prince.

And there you are:

off saving another princess,

slaying her dragons.

My dragons

are now comforting me.

Reminding me they are not

my enemies, while slowly choking

the life out of me.

Princesses

don't

have

stretch

marks.

They don't cry

themselves to sleep.

They don't watch

their prince love someone else.

They don't.

I think witches have it going

on.

They burn down kingdoms

who taught their boys

to overlook girls

who refuse to sing,

just because they said so.

They cast a spell on us

in our quiet towers.

INDEPENDENCE

A seed that blossoms

into the very thing

they have tried

to breed out of us.

The trait that clings

to a woman's bones

and turns her

from princess

to dragon.

YOU RAISED A NEW GENERATION OF WITCHES.

You waited.

And cried as you

were abused.

Did more waiting,

Did more crying,

Slayed the ~~dragon~~ prince,

Realized your power.

Burned the tower,

and saved yourself.

(AN ODE TO AMANDA LOVELACE'S

"THE PRINCESS SAVES HERSELF IN THIS ONE.")

GREEDY BOYS

Princesses don't always let

greedy boys

slip their hands

under their dresses.

But when they do,

those boys pull out their hearts.

Leaving that body feeling empty.

As if without him,

it no longer belonged to her.

STAGE FRIGHT

I choke.

My legs buckle

I forget to breathe.

I forget how to sing a single note.

I forget the words, all that's left is a ringing

in my head. A part of me hoping

to look out and see you in the crowd.

A part of me knowing I won't and cursing myself

for hoping you'll hug me

tightly afterwards.

But then I step foot on that stage.

My dragons hiss and return to their cave.

Whispering "We lost her..."

My heart is loud, and my dream is clear.

Then I blink and I'm back in my tower,

praying for a stage.

SOMETIMES PRINCES AREN'T MEANT TO SAVE YOU

Abuse isn't always a punch,

or the ripping of clothes.

It's the silent treatment
after I say no.

It's the "playful" slap

to my cheek

or the tight grip on my throat.

It's the pain that you left me with.

The pain that you said I ruined your life.

NO ONE'S WON THE WAR YET

Some days, my blood boils

and I scream at my dragons,

Banishing them back

to their caves

with their tails between
their legs.

And sometimes,

they send me to my room

with glazed eyes,

a stomach full of pills,

and an urge to tear my skin
apart.

Whispering, *"Nice try, princess.*

"YOU'RE 1 POINT AWAY"

When I found out sugar

was coursing through my body.

My heart stopped.

The headaches made sense,

you had every reason to fear.

But when I found out,

my demons tried to make

it seem like I'd be better as a bag

of bones.

PERSPECTIVE

Sometimes

I look at princesses and witches

and I realize they aren't really different.

Just two women in the world.

One who was saved.

The other who was

too ruthless to save

and too rebellious to lay down and die.

If someone told me

I was preparing you for her,

I would have locked you out.

Threw you from my tower

and pulled spikes from the ground.

Because then I didn't know

that love was pulling the twigs

from your hair.

Convincing you to stop cutting people

with the blade under your tongue.

Then hugging you

until that angry, broken, confused boy

looked at me with softened eyes.

I didn't know love was

letting you choose

a life without me, without

cursing you to hell.

I didn't know it was pushing

you toward her with a smile

on my face. A knife in my

heart. And my dragons

whispering, *"He's never*

coming back."

THE BEST GIFT YOU EVER GAVE ME.

I didn't know love was being ~~hopeful that you would~~. ~~Even when I knew there was an 85% chance you wouldn't.~~ happy for you even when you chose

to leave me to save her,

to leave me to save myself.

ODE TO MOTHER NATURE AND QUEEN WITCH.

Amanda Lovelace

taught me

to write it on a page,

Rupi Kaur

taught me

to find peace with it.

Sometimes I have the urge

to burn down this tower.

Sometimes I have the urge

to scrub it from the floorboards

to the ceiling and turn it into a home.

Sometimes I have the urge

to become a chandelier.

AT LEAST YOU DIDN'T TAKE THAT

Every month

is a constant reminder

that you left nothing

with me when you left.

And every month

I praise myself

for keeping my dress on.

BITTER TASTE

I gave you fair warning.

You proved yourself unworthy.

I gave him no warning

and he cradled me close to his heart.

Showing me all those scars,

begging me to show him mine.

When I did, he smiled

and told me how I was beautiful,

and he didn't have to remove

any article of clothing.

That was beautiful.

But now I'm left

with the bitter taste

of your kiss

and the faint memory

of my hand in his.

RAISED TO BE

I was named after two princesses,

Belle- the lover of books

who tamed a beast's wild heart,

Anastasia- the princess

who never got to experience that life.

I was named after a princess.

But I was raised to be

the knight to the princess of the house.

And I did manage to tame a beast.

But I pushed him away,

so, he could focus on a life
without me.

WHIPPED

Anastasia means to rise again.

I welcome that restart like an old friend.

Because, next time.

I'll hug you.

I'll never kiss him.

I'll never give him that job.

Next time, I'll let you go again.

Even if it stabs me in the heart.

Again.

Evil witch,

The beautiful,

The glorious,

And *oh! so special* girls

your kingdom threw away.

YOU DIDN'T LISTEN WHEN I WAS HERE

I'm done trying to shove

my story down your throat.

I'm done trying to force

you to hear me.

I have turned

my back to you.

You will beg to hear one word

from my lips when I fly

to the western sky.

Even then, you will be greeted with silence.

WHAT MAKES YOU THINK?

You didn't bother to listen

when you saw the signs.

You threatened to uproot me

from my tower and

throw me into another.

What makes you think

I will grant you entrance to my lair?

My fingers itch with ice and
fire.

Sometimes I want to burn
you

where you stand

then take your ashes

and turn you into ice.

Then I realize,

I'll be the voices in my head

and the dragons

that I'm still struggling to
tame.

I'll burn

any prince,

princess,

queen,

king,

antagonist,

protagonist,

or stable boy

who tries to lay a finger on you.

So, sleep.

I'll be your guardian angel.

I gave up

my innocence for you.

I'll give up

my life for you as well.

I inherited your anger.

Instead of throwing it back
in your face,

I spent the years mastering
the art

of expressing rage on paper.

Sometimes it does get out
of control.

Sometimes I lose the grip
and

it releases itself on my skin.

After all, I was never meant
to channel it.

I was meant to suffer from
it.

YOU MISSED THE SAPLING STAGE

I fought these battles

without you.

For years.

I mastered the art of

cracking the ground

and taking root on my own.

I learned love wasn't easy.

It required the breaking of walls.

It required trust.

It required letting yourself go.

I learned love wasn't easy or fair.

Because now I mourn for us every night.

As my blood screams,
"No one else is getting past these walls!"

PIT STOPS

Witches cry too.

The people we love hurt us too,

we love too,

we want love,

but it seems like love

doesn't want us.

We get trapped too,

except princes try to run through us

like we're pit stops.

Telling us we should be honored.

FINALLY

I wish you would have told me.

That you intended to have me

as part of your body count.

But then again,

I'm glad you didn't.

Because my heart is finally on my side.

THESE DRAGONS AND THOSE DRAGONS

You know how in the last book

I talked about dragon blood?

These dragons

and those dragons

aren't the same.

Like flour

and flower

aren't the same.

It's all about the context.

RELEASING

Puberty hit you like a truck.

And I was the only one there to help.

I saw the dragon in you.

It just broke my heart

that I had to add you

to the long list of people

Who used me to release their rage.

THAT NIGHT

I poured my heart

out to the stars.

As I wept,

they slept.

And that night

I tore the sky apart.

Vowing to never again

whisper my secrets

to the wind.

Everyone

I ever looked up to

showed me

They're just another person
in the world,

Trying to make it through.

Looking for someone

to look up to.

SCHUYLER SISTERS.

Eliza deserved to be loved

even when she was away.

Angelica deserved to find a soul

as untamed as hers.

Peggy deserved to be noticed

for the angel she was.

ANOTHER THING I COULDN'T CONTROL

I never wanted to hurt you.

Apparently,

you

didn't

feel

the

same

way.

THE MASTERING OF SILENCE

My life has consisted

of biting my own tongue off.

Swallowing it.

Watching it regrow

Slowly,

with every cruel word

a child shouldn't hear.

Repeat.

I never meant

to ruin your life.

But I'm not sorry.

You knew you were
touching soft clay.

It's not my fault

you pushed harder than
others

and left your mark

for all to see.

I forgive you,

But the ones after you may not.

The ones before you don't.

He spent years chipping

at the brick,

and you came in

and smashed them down

without my consent.

I mistook that hunger

for some kind of affection.

Then, I saw it.

Now, you've landed

on the spikes at the bottom.

And he? He's hanging on.

I forgive you, but the ones after you

may not. And now you left them

with another dragon to tame.

TRYING TO FALL OUT OF IT

I am in the process of
breaking.

The slow, agonizing process of
breaking.

The kind that cracks over time,

where some days I love you.

Some days, I want to burn you

to the ground,

so you'll never hurt me
again.

Some days I want to let you
hug me

without withdrawing
emotionally.

Some days my skin screams for you

to let me go.

(Some days I miss him so much

my bones can't take it

and I want to do whatever it takes).

Then all the R.H. Sin poems

I've ever read remind me

I shouldn't have to fight

for you to choose me.

And those nights, those nights... I break.

All over a what if.

And a necklace I purposely lost.

Stable boy,

How I am waiting

for you to love

these broken parts.

How I am praying

I've already met you.

I just want someone

to call me beautiful

while looking directly

in my eyes.

I want my soul to shake,

not my legs, with desire.

I want my heart to shake

in fear of him.

I want to hear God speak

so clearly that it drowns

out my thoughts.

I want to hear him say,

"You're welcome.

I made this one for you."

A LIFE BEFORE

I don't want my daughter chasing boys

in their carriages full of women.

I want her to live before boys.

I want her to see Hawaii before boys.

I want her to learn

about heart break before that boy.

Because then she'll realize.

I lived before you.

I will live after you.

I loved before you.

I'll love after you.

I felt before you.

I'll feel after you.

AND I HOPE YOU GET THROUGH

My heart weeps

for the next boy

who tries to claim this heart.

Because I know

I will burn,

I was scratch,

I will kick and fight,

I will push you, and I will push you hard.

Because my dragons

will come ready to attack.

Smirking, "*Go ahead and try.*"

#THEDUMBWANNABE POET

I wish R.H Sin had reached me sooner.

But, thank you

for reaching out

in the first place.

A SECRET

I want to share

my poetry

with you

but I am afraid

that is too intimate

I let my numbness

take your spot.

Maybe that's when

the hand you held

turned to ice

and the other burned

to a crisp.

THE ART OF GROWING UP

I kissed blades

before I kissed boys.

I think that's when I lost it.

GLAD I DIDN'T

His ghost haunts every room.

Every. Single. Room.

Except mine.

I refused to let that prince

exist inside these walls.

Now the thought of you

makes me smirk,

Because I'm not so sad

that I frown

And I'm not so star-struck

that I lose my self-control.

You're a sweet memory

that left a bitter after-taste.

INVITE ME IN

I just want someone

who will come,

offering me nothing but his hand.

Not a teddy bear,

or a necklace,

or diamond studded earrings.

I want you to come with your palm upward.

I want you to not surrender to me.

But to invite me in,

To allow us to coexist with

each other.

I want to be the person who helps you use a bow as you teach me how to handle it without a weapon.

I want my demons to shake in fear when you step over the threshold of my heart. I want them to back into the corner, petrified.

I want to do the same for yours.

I can't fix them, but I can try to help you

keep them at bay.

MY HAPPY ENDING

I don't want a castle.

I want a cottage away from
the world.

Away from the queens,

And the dragons

(the ones we can

escape from anyway).

The kings,

princes & princesses

who were never worthy

of our troubled, but
beautiful hearts.

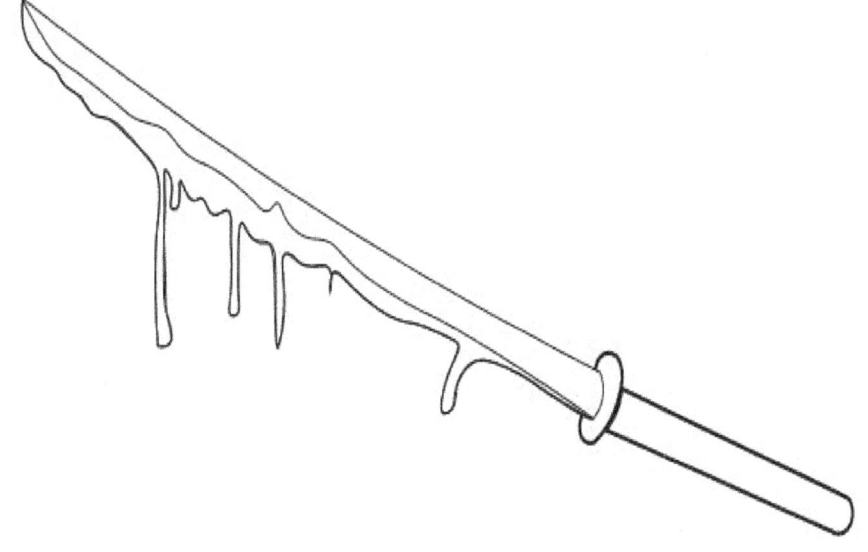

The Salem witch trials never ended.

We just made

pretty boys our **princes**.

But my dear the moment you realize you don't need him you will be called a witch.

Welcome to the coven.

This was never

to ruin your name.

But only to warn people

about the kind of people

who are connected to kings.

SELF-DESTRUCTION

Alexander

ruined

everything

because he wouldn't say no.

Why is there a thrill

that comes

with self-destruction?

YOU DIED

I won't lie

and say

I don't miss you.

I won't lie

and say

I don't sometimes

blame myself.

But if you ask,

I will look you in the eye

and walk away.

I have nothing to say to a ghost.

STEAK

I don't like

the way

you watched

me shrink

into

my hoodie.

THE SHEEP AND THE WOLF

You sat in the corner

and watched every move I made.

I made every move

so carefully

that I forgot to breathe.

BURN TO FORGET YOU

I remembered when we danced.

I set that part of my brain aflame.

Every now and then I open the door

to see if you still reside there.

Then when I see you sitting on the couch,

I set myself aflame.

If I must burn to forget you,

then I will repeat history.

TEENAGE NONSENSE

I saw you

swoop her up

once he left.

He called you friend.

You called him the ex.

She called you the rebound.

I called it pathetic.

I WANT TO FORGET

Skin cells live for about 2 weeks.

The generations before them must have described in explicit detail

what your touch was like.

How your jacket felt,

what your kiss was like,

how your hand felt in mine.

They must have written it down word for word from the mouth of the source.

WHAT COULD I HAVE DONE?

Sometimes,

I want to go bang on your door
and ask why.

Sometimes I hover over your
contact, prepared to scream
and demand answers.

Now I let it go.

I let it fly into the wind,
because now

I no longer care why.

I no longer want to waste my
time

dreaming about how I could
avoid it.

Because I've learned

It's hard to avoid.

It's hard to remove yourself
from an election you never
knew you were part of.

FORGIVENESS

has entered the chat

"Hey"

not delivered

I COULDN'T STAY QUIET THE SECOND TIME AROUND

At your funeral, I buried you.

At your funeral, I read your eulogy to the empty seats.

At your funeral, you took my peace of mind with you in the ground.

I didn't cry at the funeral; I cried the morning after.

I threw up all your lies,

your words came up like hair balls.

That love came up like the aftermath of food poisoning.

That morning I looked up from my piano and saw you.

And it all came out.

I danced with the devil.

The devil danced with me.

I don't think he understood the mistake

he made trying to go toe-to-toe with untapped energy

SAVE YOURSELF

Princes aren't always good.

They aren't always kind and loving.

Sometimes they love you.

Sometimes they don't.

Sometimes they hurt you,

but let's pray that they won't.

But if they do,

do not be afraid.

Because, witches run in the family.

I told myself after you,

I'd find myself again.

Over 3 months later I've now realized.

I don't know who she is.

Because I lost her long before you.

At least I say I lost her.

Because, that's easier than saying I believe that maybe I was born hollow.

AN ACT OF SELF DEFENSE

You don't get to say you
ruined my innocence.

It was gone before you.

It's disgusting that you knew
that.

Yet you still charged and left
me with no choice

but to break your neck.

I FORGIVE YOU

I pray you don't forget what you did.

I pray you forgive yourself.

Because I have seen

what guilt and grief does to people.

I'd hate to have to host another funeral.

We got greedy.

You took it too far.

I locked myself away in my tower again.

I forgave you.

The end.

DISCLAIMER

There will be no sequel.

IT STUCK, YOU KNOW

You were both important.

You both burned me.

But the first burn stuck.

LEARN

Forgiveness

doesn't mean you get to come back.

If you shoot me and I survive,

then hand you another gun, fully loaded,

That's no longer a mistake.

That's suicide.

AWAY FROM PRINCES LIKE YOU

The birds don't sing songs about you.

I don't know what color your hair is

or how long it is.

If it's buzzed, or curly, or in braids.

The wind doesn't carry you to me.

Instead, the ground broke between your part

of the woods and mine.

You stay in your kingdom.

I stay in my cottage

away from princes like you

and I think that's for the best.

BUT I'M NOT AFRAID OF IT.

I haven't gone back

to the crime scene.

THE ART OF LETTING IT DIE.

I held another funeral.

I laid us down 100 feet apart.

I laid down our friendship, the love I had for my friend, the nonexistent love I had for that boyfriend, the trust, the relationship, I laid down the pictures, and the text messages.

I laid us down. I smiled and whispered, "die." They seeped into the ground and grew a flower.

Beautiful to look at and poisonous to touch.

That's what we were.

Every now and then I bring flowers.

Not to keep us alive.

But to mourn the way our book ended and seek inspiration from a love story gone wrong.

THE END

I hope you move on.

I hope you grow old and happy.

I hope you find a woman

who soothes your broken heart.

I hope you tell your children

about the kinds of things people do in the dark.

I no longer see you as what you've done.

I see your potential to raise a generation of royalty.

I pray you find peace writing

another story somewhere else.

But if the wind and the
sunflowers tell me

of you repeating history.

I will come walking.

A **king** doesn't earn his title
by

how many kingdoms he
overthrows.

He earns it by teaching
princes how

to be kings.

THE TEACHINGS OF A KING

I live in the same house as a king.

And, he's taught me that a king

is just a man.

Who made it his business

to provide, care, and love his family.

My father is the standard.

Point. Blank.

Period.

TEACHINGS OF MY DAD

My dad taught me

sometimes silence is the best response in anger.

Walking away doesn't make you

a coward. Leaving does.

My dad taught me to bow my head in respect

without groveling in submission.

My dad taught me

how to acknowledge the difference

between a king and a boy.

He taught me the standard.

A LESSON I MISSED.

My dad never taught me

about boys until it was too late.

I wish he did.

To all the sperm donors and incubators who walked out on their kids.

Burn.

To all the parents who raised the kids on their own.

I applaud you.

To the kids who are trying to get through life without them.

You'll be fine.

I believe in you.

SOME ADVICE

To the men trying to be

the father they never had.

Here's some advice.

Do everything he never did,

that you wish he did.

I LEARNED FROM YOU

I never knew the value of a father.

Until I met people who had a father.

Then lost him.

COPING MECHANISM

My father poured into me

the one thing that

has kept me alive this far.

Music.

READ MY EYES

I still see it in your eye

Sometimes, when you look at me.

I can see the disappointment in yourself,

the misplaced guilt.

I can see the apology for letting me down.

Read my eyes: "It's okay."

NOTHING ELSE

Sometimes I want to cry in my dad's arms

and tell him.

Tell him

how you broke

his little girl's heart.

But I smile because I don't know what else to do.

I watch in awe

As you burn the title

the world has placed upon you.

Because, you are content with

being the random **maiden** in their story.

The wild soul they could never buy.

Maidens aren't witches,

Or evil queens,

Or princesses.

They are the girls

who war for themselves

when no one else will.

LINE UP

I put on

my armor

and fight

for my own hand.

ROLE MODEL

I saw your demons

try to overrun you.

I saw you wield your sword

and stand up ready to fight.

I like that.

MY DAILY REMINDER

"It has to get better.

This can't be it."

PERSPECTIVE II

Tears sting.

It's like our body's way of punishing us

for showing we feel things.

Or,

It's our body reminding us

that we are still feeling things.

You know. Like we are still alive

and that sometimes that's all we can ask for.

I didn't fall out of _____ I jumped.

Because I knew I needed to stop.

AN OAK TREE AND A BLADE OF GRASS

I used to raise my voice

to get you to listen to reason.

You'd grovel in the corner

shaking from just me being assertive.

TALKING TO MY PEERS

When will we stop

looking for love

in one-night stands?

NATIVES

I had never felt

like such a European

on my own land.

I love seeing girls

with hair as bright

as the sun.

BURN THE TITLE

I'm watching women

wearing their scars

like pageant sashes.

That's how I know,

I was born

for this new era of women.

POETRY MAKES PEOPLE FEEL THINGS.

I wet my fingers and dragged them along the ink.

When my fingertips came back black.

I felt your story soak into my skin.

I realized my story was never meant to be

stuck on mere pages.

It was meant to be

stuck to your bones.

It was meant to be felt by your heart.

WE SAW IT COMING

She broke your heart.

Now you are sitting here

sobbing over an idea.

We all sit back and sigh.

Because we saw ash

falling from the sky.

While you saw flecks of gold.

STAND YOUR GROUND

Stop answering.

Say your goodbyes.

Choke every bird who comes

baring a message from them.

Scream.

Cry.

Listen to your sad songs.

Cry.

Burn that bridge. They no

longer deserve

a way to get close to your

heart.

Pack up your stuff and leave that town.

Stand your ground

when you hear about the new girl.

Wish her luck.

HOW TO LET GO

Keep

it pushing.

Once again

I was told

to swallow my story.

I now live in fear

of all the girls

we might lose

because I decided

to be obedient.

READ CAREFULLY

Here's the thing about depression people don't get.

~~The gym does not help, it does not get rid of the gnawing and the scratching.~~

~~Depression doesn't care, it will happen at church, a funeral, a wedding, a party, a movie, a gym, and in your house.~~

Depression doesn't care about you.

SPIRITUAL WARFARE

I knew I was strong

when I dropped to my knees

and prayed for you.

A THIRST

When I was younger,

I thought poetry was for the weak.

I thought being emotional and letting

your words be heard was a sign of weakness.

Now I hunt for those books,

and when I see them my mouth starts drooling.

FLOW

Poetry and music

flow through my blood.

I'm the embodiment of
sound.

Heartbreak

of some kind

has influenced

75% of my poetry.

SHOW ME

Some days I want someone

to tell me I'm worthy of love.

Some days I want someone to show me.

Most days I have to question

if my heart can take another heart break.

OUR SECRETS

One summer I want to disappear

with my best friends

and not come back until fall.

Then I want to tell no one

where we went

or what we did.

TRUTH

If it doesn't resonate

in your soul.

Then it's not poetry.

A SPLIT SECOND

I want to sing into the night sky.

I want to see if my songs will reach heaven.

Maybe if I break the barrier for a split second,

I'll remember the smell of holy oil.

Maybe, I'll get a glimpse of what I'm reaching for.

MYTH:

Perfect daughters exist.

When a king dies,

why is it still called a Kingdom?

It's no longer his.

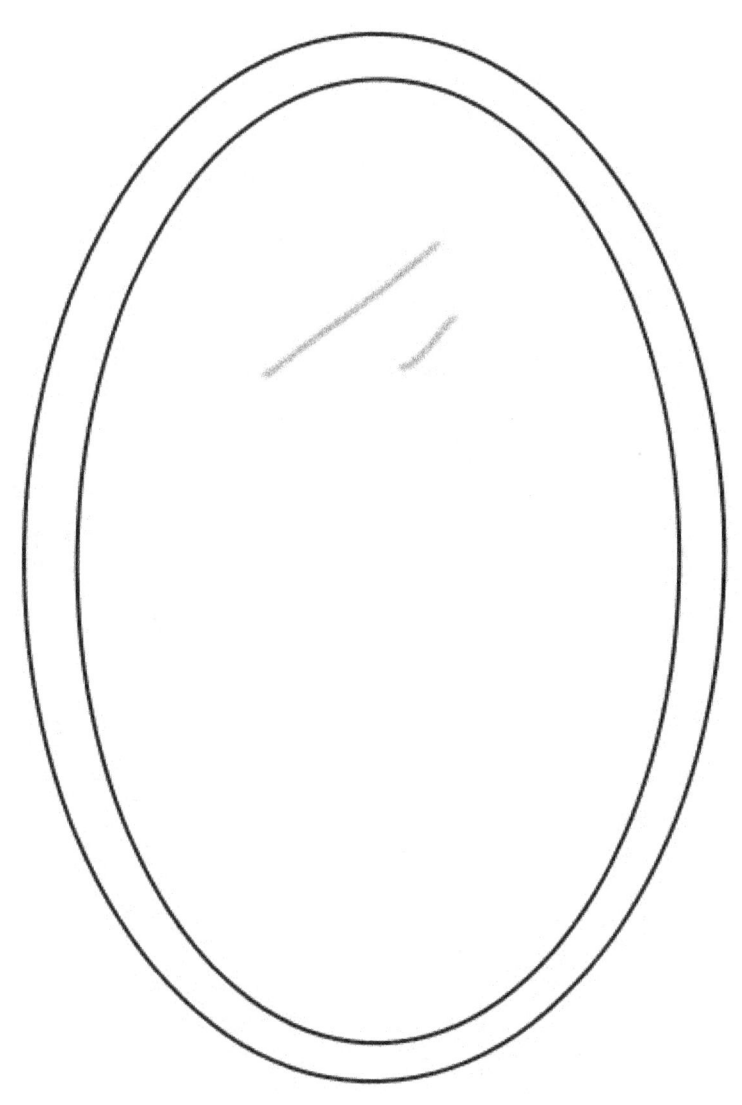

The **truth** is going

to set you free.

Only if you are willing

To give up on the fairytales

they fed us as babes.

WORDS MATTER

The Grimm Brothers knew
real life.

We dumbed it down for the
child.

Now your daughter is calling
a wolf her friend.

While you're bleeding out in
the closet.

Wishing you had told her
the truth.

CINDERELLA

Cinderella was a witch who hid from a prince.

Her stepsisters were ultimately disgusting.

Her stepmother was awful.

There was no fairy Godmother. There was only a tree.

Now, as Cinderella gets married, the wicked sisters get their eyes poked out.

Teach your kids not to be wicked.

Teach them not to be liars.

So they don't get their eyes poked out.

SNOW WHITE

The evil queen wanted to eat

Snow-White's lungs and liver.

After three times of trying

to kill Snow White she gives her the apple.

(you know how that part goes)

The prince wants to bury her in the ground.

They trip and fall (like clumsy men do)

And Snow-White coughs up

a piece of apple.

Then, they force the Evil Queen to dance in hot iron shoes at the wedding until she dies.

Boys shouldn't kiss dead girls because that's weird.

Sometimes revenge turns you into the evil one.

MYTH:

I'm over it.

MYTH:

I don't miss you.

MYTH:

I don't relapse.

BEAUTY'S WICKED SISTERS

Some girls don't care

whether they lie in captivity

or are free.

As long as they have

a pearl necklace around their neck.

MYTH:

I don't cry at night.

MYTH:

I'm perfect.

MYTH (MY BROKEN SPELL):

I must be perfect.

I must be perfect.

I must be perfect.

I must be perfect.

I must be perfect.

I must be perfect.

MYTH:

I'm sure on how to feel.

I'm not sure on what's true.

All I know is

people are only as perfect

as we make them.

EVERYONE HURTS (USED AS A VERB OR NOUN)

"People have hurt you

and they weren't just boys.

Girls too, women you've trusted."

SOMETHING ISN'T BEING SAID

I feel like there's something

off in the gene pool.

Because I keep seeing a glitch

in the women around me.

NO LOVE AMONG SISTERS.

Boys broke my heart.

But girls,

girls made me hollow.

"Fat"

"Ugly"

"Look at her…"

Who told us it was our jobs

to bring each other down?

SHAME

My sisters,

we stand together during
rallies for our rights,

but we hold one another's
head

under the water

over a boy who likes boys.

BODY COUNT

I don't know why

my generation thrives

on how many people

we've hurt.

There's something about looking for

refuge in your peers,

only to be cast out

because you refuse to drink

from the fountain

that turned them into monsters.

CLEAN YOUR MIRROR

How do you get rid

of the problem?

How do you leave it

behind you

when it shows up

in your mirror?

It's so stupid

how we war

against each other

because of what he said…

WORTH HOLDING ON

I hold on.

I hold onto pain.

I hold onto good.

I hold onto to and try to

mold it into something else.

But sometimes, it's too much to bear on my own.

I want to want someone.

I also want to know

if I can't have that person,

the sun will still rise,

the world will still spin,

and I will still be worthy of love.

I KNOW BETTER

I don't want to be needed,

Because so many people are already screaming,

they need me.

It makes me feel like if I waver,

I am no better than a drunk father

who destroys himself in front of his children

and doesn't blink twice.

They are already pulling my
skin off my bones

and I stand tall and it is all
because she needs me.

I can't be the alcohol parent

who is too selfish

to get her life together

for the sake of her child.

ASKING WHY

Sometimes my mouth runs, untangling itself and finally feeling free to say what it's been hiding.

I beg it to slow down.

Give me a second.

Let me write it down.

But it runs, and runs, and runs circles around me.

My own body that I abused turning against me because I kept it locked away.

But when I scream "Write,"

My tongue sits down and stares at me.

We just look at each other and ask "Why?

Why?

Why am I needed?

Why do you run to me

begging for my body?

Taking my body like bread.

Taking me before you'll take God.

Trying to drag me to the cross

and beating me because, I am only human.

Beating me because, I am just like you.

You come to me and

bring your collection of problems.

You love me when I take those problems

and carry them.

But, when you come forward

and see that my hands are

gashed open,

My eyes are glazed over,

my knees are buckling,

and I am bleeding

from every ounce of my body,

You circle me like a crow

as I beg for forgiveness for being human.

You see the knives in my back

and add your own to the mix.

You grab me by my throat and spit in my face.

"You're no God."

I cry because finally

you understood what

I've been trying to tell you

since the beginning.

Then you come back, and I
dry my eyes.

STILL TRYING TO FIGURE IT OUT

God, what is this?

Why?

Why did you make me

so capable

to carry their problems and

mine?

Why couldn't you make

me fragile and weak

so that way the outside

would match how my insides

feel?

YOU DID IT

You already imbedded your
rage inside me.

There's nothing more you
can do

than beg for mercy

from the flames you
sparked.

SOME THINGS I DON'T KNOW

There's something about that ache.

That burn.

That need.

That urge to run.

To run and not look back.

I never understood it.

It washes over me and holds me.

Screaming for me to run

before it's too late.

Telling me I can't keep these

parts secret forever.

But I plug my headphones in

and blow my eardrums
apart.

Looking it in the face and
smirking.

I'm not sure if I'm the villain
in that story.

JEALOUSY

I realized that

people will hate

the decisions you made.

Simply because they wish

that they had made

that decision before you.

VILLAINS

I hope I'm not the villain in your story.

Yes, you.

Because I'm going to let you read this one.

Hundreds of miles away from me though.

But nonetheless, I hope you're proud of this progress.

But if I'm the villain give me a cape

and a dope musical number.

If I'm the Evil Queen,

then I hope you see me blush

as you bash my name.

If anyone asks me

"Was he the prince?

Did he save you from the dragon?"

I'll probably shrug as my heart breaks a little bit.

"No, he was just a boy."

"Then what were you?"

"I was just a dumb girl

chasing after a dumb boy."

"So, there was no dragon?"

"No... there was definitely a dragon.

But we didn't kill it. I actually think it killed us."

AGE

I have an older sister.

Who I love dearly.

But I need a big sister.

Who could have warned me

about people who would hurt me.

So that way I wouldn't be 15

feeling 30, looking 20

Waiting for the end like 80.

Giving advice to 18 like I'm 48.

God isn't a woman.

God made women

with his breath and his hands.

That alone makes me feel powerful.

REALIZING

I remember

when I used to blame God

for everything people said.

For everything people did to me.

Now, I fall on my knees and cry.

Asking Him to forgive me

for blaming the coach

for what the players

on the opposite team did.

GOD ANSWERS

I remember when I asked
my dad,

"Why is committing suicide
a sin?"

I had never seen

my dad waver

until that moment.

Then the car smelled like
holy oil

and I heard a voice.

"Because, I'm not done
making you."

APOSTLE ROY SHEARS

"You don't come to church

because you've got it all right.

You come to church

because you're trying to get it right."

I CAN SMELL IT

Whenever I smell holy oil in the air.

I get excited.

I know

something good

is happening.

HE FORGIVES

God called a man

with the blood of his followers

on his hands.

He called him to preach

to the people

who he once murdered.

So why do we scream,

"God can't forgive what I did"?

Something about death

makes my bones shake

in fear

of getting to the gates

and being met with a frown

and a fire on my tail.

WHY AM I LIKE THIS?

When I find my room become dirty.

I find myself searching through socks.

Then I find myself screaming because one sock is stretched out and chewed up by my dog.

Then I'm tripping over my dirty leggings.

Then I notice my room is becoming dirty.

And I remember that *your room*

is a representation of your mind.

So, I drop to my knees

putting all my dirty clothes
in the basket

ready for a wash.

Fixing my bed and tucking
the sheets back into place.

I gasp a breath of fresh air.

I sit down to admire my
handiwork.

Then I see that same
stretched sock.

And somehow now there's a
giant hole

where my heel goes.

IT BE LIKE THAT.

2018 broke me down.

Kicked me around.

And knocked my lights out.

But sometimes it be like that.

Acknowledgments

To my grandma,

HGTV will never be the same without you.

To Tebit,

thank you for never leaving me.

To Josh,

thank you for existing.

To my Flower Child,

I love you and your Aries chaos.

To me a year ago,

Thank you for staying alive.

I think we're almost out of the woods.

Social Media

- Website:
  www.StaziaBelle.com

- Instagram:
  StaziaBelle

- Twitter:
  StaziaBelle

www.ingramcontent.com/pod-product-compliance
Lightning Source LLC
Chambersburg PA
CBHW071455040426
42444CB00008B/1355